Grammaropolis
PRESENTS

Connie the Conjunction

Written by Coert Voorhees
Illustrations by Powerhouse Animation

Meet the Parts of Speech

I name a specific person, place, thing, or idea. It's a big responsibility, naming things—a responsibility that requires a certain attention to detail.

Nelson the Noun

Some people say I'm all over the place. Some people call me a ball of energy. I take that as a compliment, because I just like to go, go, go!

Vinny the Action Verb

I take the place of one or more Nouns or Pronouns. I always want the Noun's job, and I hang out with the Verb and Adjective.

Roger the Pronoun

I'm perfectly happy to link Nouns and Pronouns with the appropriate Adjectives, but it's not like I'm going to expend a lot of energy doing so.

Lucy the Linking Verb

I modify a Noun or Pronoun. I tell what kind, which one, how many, or how much. I pride myself on being the most artistic of the parts of speech.

Jake the Adjective

Gather 'round everybody and let's have ourselves a wonderful time. I just love bringing words and groups of words together, don't you?

Connie the Conjunction

I modify a Verb, Adjective, or other Adverb. I tell how, when, where, to what extent, and under what condition. I often end in –ly, but I don't have to.

Benny the Adverb

I express emotion!! Yep, I'm always here, always ready with my commas and exclamation points, just in case.

Izzy the Interjection

They call me Preposition because I'm pre-positioned. I'm first. At the front. Before every other word in the phrase? Got it?

Li'l Pete the Preposition

I am a chameleon. A spy. An undercover operative. I infiltrate the sentence and act as whatever part of speech suits me.

Slang

CONNIE THE CONJUNCTION

© 2019 Grammaropolis

Graphic Design by Mckee Frazior

Text and Illustrations © 2011 by Grammaropolis LLC

This book is typeset in Komika Text

Distributed throughout the world by Ingram Publisher Services
www.ingrambook.com

Everyone trusted Connie's taste.

If her customers ever fought over an item, she made sure they got along.

She loved all the conjunctions, but her favorites were the coordinating conjunctions. She called them "FANBOYS" for short.

6

She could use one of the FANBOYS to link two phrases.
I recommend choosing the striped shirt or the polka-dot pants.
or
Coordinating Conjunctions
for and nor but or yet so

Connie could even use one of the FANBOYS to link two independent clauses.

One day, Jake was so proud of his new outfit that he forgot to mop the wet floor.

I am dashing, charming...

10

Connie felt a little dizzy, but she jumped up and got right back to work.

Lucy, I've changed my mind. Take the skirt **and** those boots **and** that jacket.

She needed something stronger.

Storage Closet

In case of emergency BREAK GLASS

Subordinating Conjunctions

Correlative Conjunctions

16

First she tried correlative conjunctions. She used them to link words and word groups used in exactly the same way.

The correlative conjunctions helped, but even they weren't quite strong enough.

She brought out the subordinating conjunctions, which she used to introduce subordinate clauses.

Putting a subordinating conjunction at the beginning of the clause made the clause dependent, which meant that it couldn't stand on its own.

Whenever I see you in those pants, I giggle.

I suggest you go back to your old look even though I like that shirt.

Functions of Conjunctions

CONJUNCTIONS

A conjunction joins words *or* word groups. Yes, indeed!

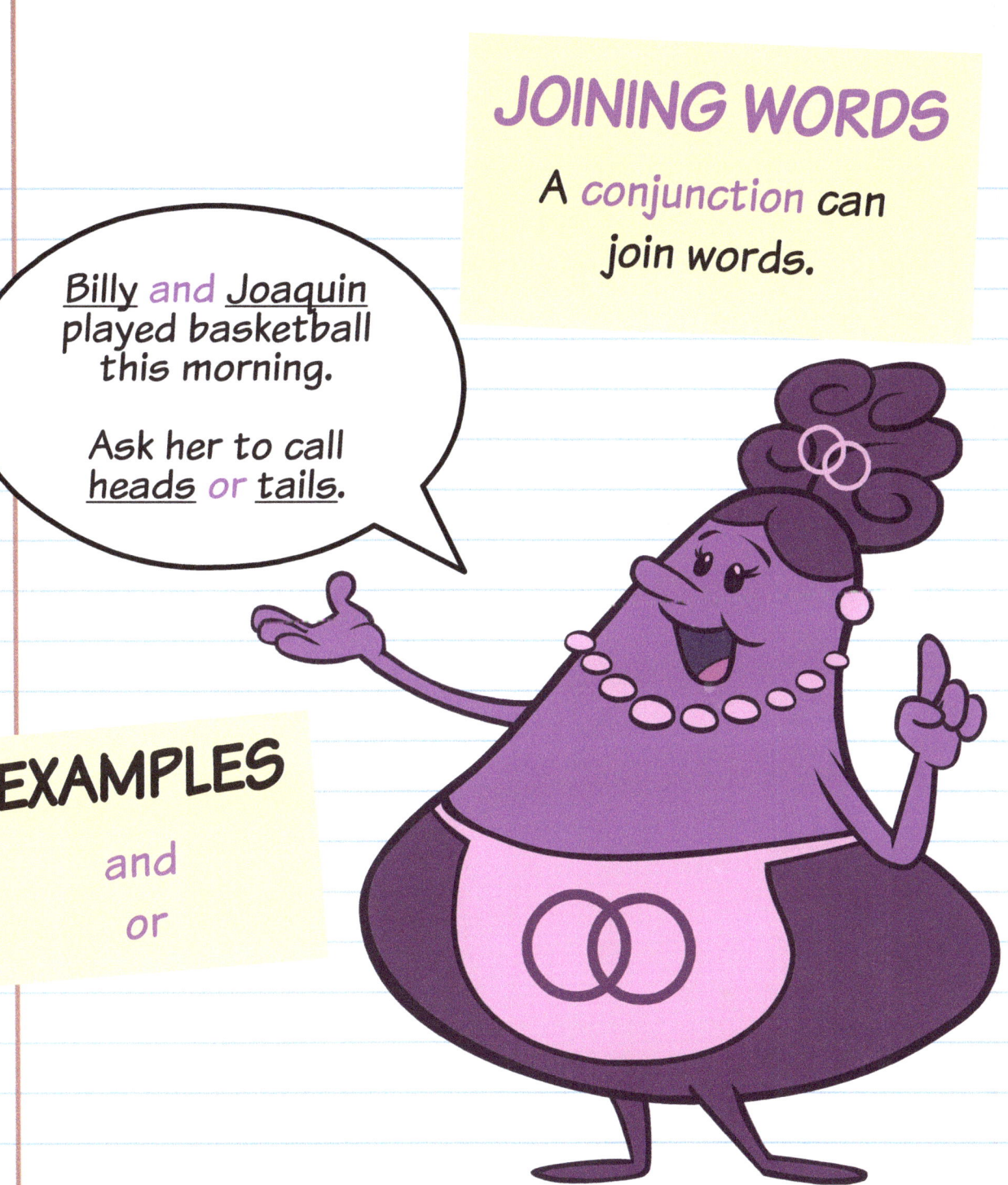

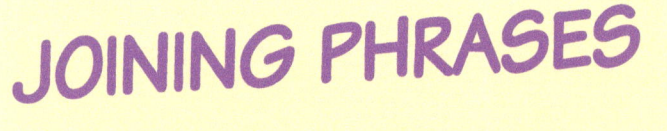

JOINING PHRASES

A conjunction can join phrases.

I keep my treasure <u>under the bed</u> or <u>in a box</u>.

Penguins have <u>white bellies</u> and <u>black wings</u>.

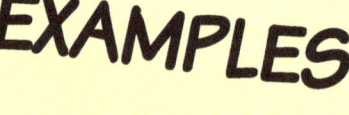

EXAMPLES

and

or

A *conjunction* can join clauses.

Nelson's platypus won't bite **unless** the moon is full.

Sarah told me a funny joke, **and** I laughed for five minutes!

EXAMPLES

unless

and

COORDINATING CONJUNCTIONS

A *coordinating conjunction* is used to join words, phrases, or independent clauses.

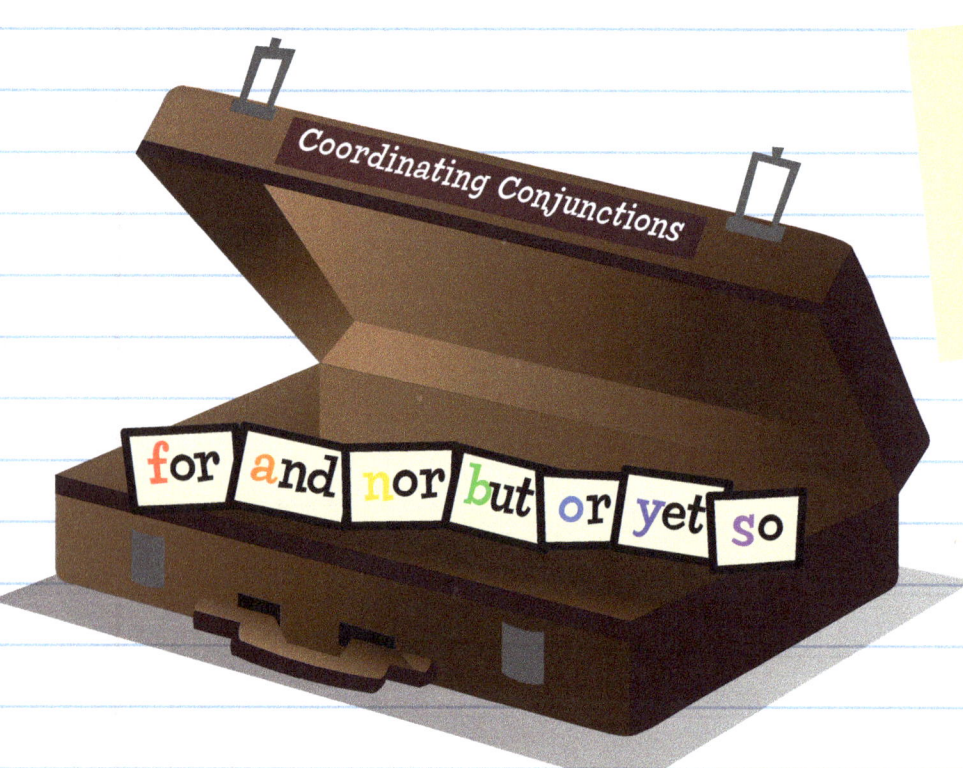

Coordinating Conjunctions

for and nor but or yet so

WORDS

Albert's sister just gave me <u>milk</u> **and** <u>cookies</u>.

PHRASES

Would you prefer to live <u>in the city</u> or <u>in the country</u>?

INDEPENDENT CLAUSES

<u>My grandfather is very old</u>, yet <u>he looks just like me</u>.

FANBOYS:
for, and, nor, but, or, yet, so

SUBORDINATING CONJUNCTIONS

A *subordinating conjunction* introduces a subordinate (dependent) clause, which is a group of words with a subject and predicate that doesn't make sense on its own.

The streets were flooded <u>because</u> it rained so hard.

<u>Wherever</u> my brother goes, people tell him he looks like a hermit crab.

EXAMPLES

because

Wherever

CORRELATIVE CONJUNCTIONS

A *correlative conjunction* is a two-part conjunction used to join words or phrases used in the same way.

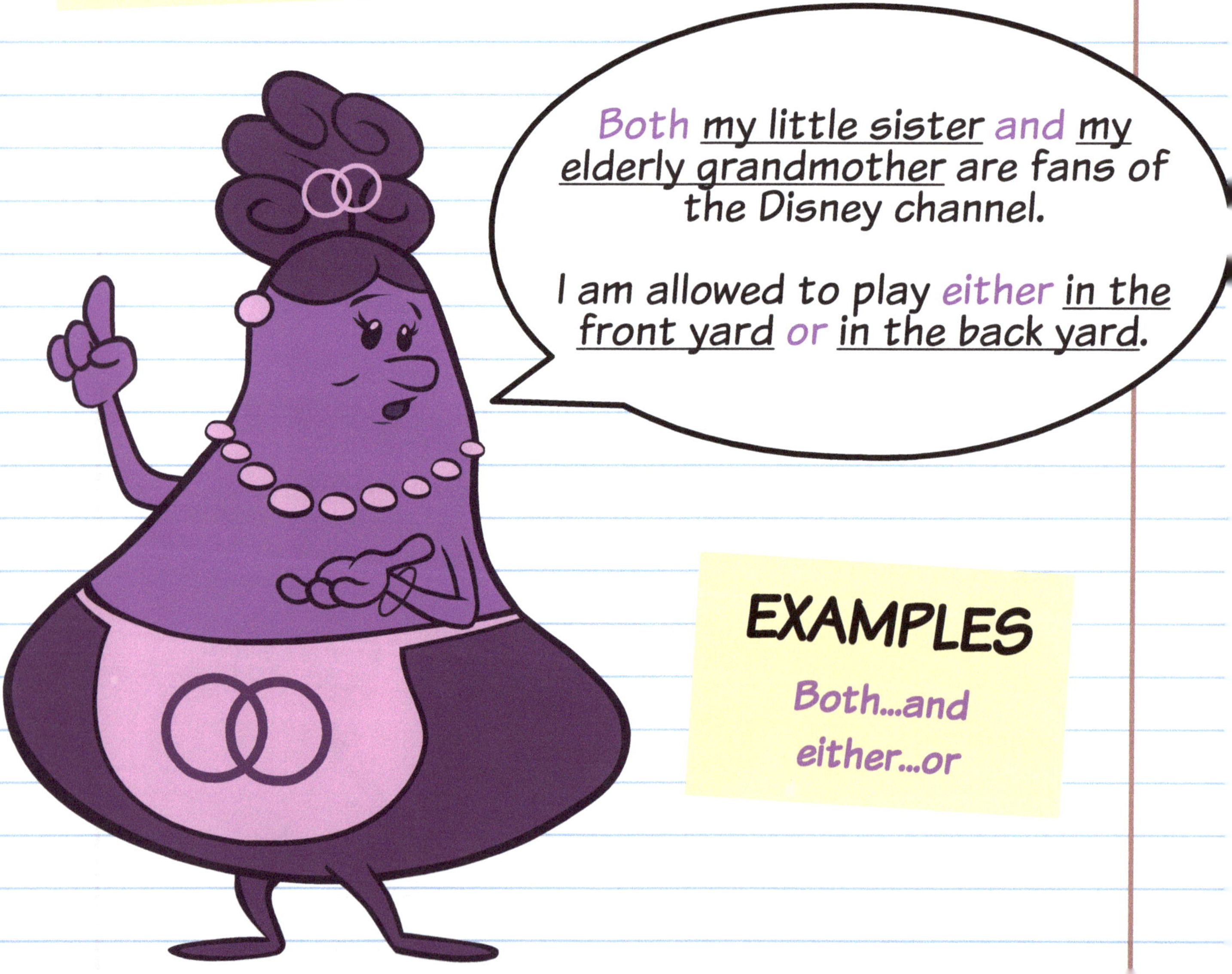

Both <u>my little sister</u> and <u>my elderly grandmother</u> are fans of the Disney channel.

I am allowed to play *either* <u>in the front yard</u> *or* <u>in the back yard.</u>

EXAMPLES

Both...and

either...or